A Ring of Roses

Book, Music and Lyrics

Darren Vallier

Jasper Publishing

1 Broad Street Hemel Hempstead Herts HP2 5BW
Tel: 01442 263461 Fax: 01442 217102

Jasper Publishing
1 Broad Street Hemel Hempstead Herts HP2 5BW
Tel: 01442 263461 Fax: 01442 217102

ISBN 1 874009 20 1

British Library Cataloguing-in-Publication Data.
A catalogue record for this book is available from
The British Library

Music score for this work is available from the same publisher under the reference
ISBN 1 874009 50 3

A superb 'Original Cast Recording' CD
of the songs is available at £12

A Ring of Roses

Book, Music and Lyrics
by
Darren Vallier

The year is 1665, the time of the Plague. Alone on the hill stand the children, isolated from their village where their parents sit waiting for the day when it will be safe to be reunited.

For the children it is a time for adventure, a time to build friendships and confront fears... it is a time when the story is told and the last word given.

It is not a time to die, just a time for letting go.

"This is simply a story of courage"

THE SETTING

The setting and the characters in this musical play are fictional. It is set in and around a small farming village just outside London. Scenes take place on a hill, in the village and at various meeting places including a stream, a bridge and the village gates.

A raked stage could be used to give the effect of height and if possible, the acting area could also include a fence, logs, a stile, plenty of leaves and sticks on the ground and a separate cobbled area with upright wooden structures of house fronts as a representation of the village. Different acting areas should be dictated by lighting.

The language used by the characters in 'A Ring of Roses' has been 'updated' to convey an identification with the events.

Musical vamps should be used at appropriate times in the script.

Any number of performers may be used to represent the characters in
'A Ring of Roses'

REFERENCES

A great deal of research was carried out into reports of the plague that swept much of England in 1665 with special reference to the factual and semi-fictional works based on the village of Eyam.

**'A Ring of Roses' was first performed at
The Gardner Arts Theatre, Brighton, June 1995
under its previous title of 'The Children of Winter'.**

**It was then performed again as 'A Ring of Roses'
in its current format at
The Connaught Theatre, Worthing, February1997,
followed by a performance at
The Savoy Theatre, London, May 1997**

Some Press Comments

'*A superb show*' Tony Wade, NODA review

'*There can't be anything to match 'A Ring of Roses*'
Derek Jameson, BBC 2

'*Deserves the wide acclaim*' Adam Kenwright, London Producer

'*I can't remember so much fuss being made... since Blood Brothers*'
Tasmin Smith The Evening Argus

'*I felt I was watching musical theatre in the West End*'
Anthony Reed (original cast of 'Jolson')

'*A fine writing talent*' Charles Vance, Amateur Stage

THE CHARACTERS

The children on the hill
These characters will wear farming rags in 'earthy' colours.
They will have dirty faces and barefeet or boots

Emily	A young girl, intelligent and articulate.
Abby	A young girl who misses her parents.
Catherine	An older girl who is in love with Thomas.
Thomas	An older boy from the village.
Alice	An older girl who everyone looks up to.
Peter	The bully!
Geoffrey	A nervous boy who suffers from imaginary illnesses.
Roland	Peter's friend. Always hungry.
Gilbert	Roland's friend but smarter than Roland.
Sheldon	The mad boy, scruffy and dirty.

Marjoram	] Three local village hags (The Sisters of Thyme)
Lichen	] dressed in black with wild hair and black teeth
Dill	] They do not get on

Jenkins	An older gravedigger. Greedy and rather abrupt. Constantly scratching and has several black, rotten teeth.
Unwin	An apprentice gravedigger, not very bright. Younger than Jenkins.
Mother	Abby's mother. Stays in village, constantly worrying.
Stranger	A mysterious yet friendly male. Appears in Act 2.

Children Chorus	Any number can be used to represent the children on the hill. There are a couple of speaking parts.
Village Chorus	Any number can be used but there are several speaking parts.

A Ring of Roses

The Songs

ACT ONE

They Will Be Who They Will Be	Solo Villager and Full Company
Where Are You Now?	Mother and Abby
A Little Bit of Spit	The Three Hags
Falling Down	Full Company
Dig Another Hole	Gravediggers and few Village Chorus
Try	Catherine and Children
I'll Be Here Waiting For You (preview)	Thomas
Where's My Dinner?	Roland, Children and Hags
See This Plague	Village Chorus, Hags and Gravediggers
Goodnight Children	Mother, Abby and Village Chorus

ACT TWO

Let Them Cry	Full Company
Still Hear The Sound Of The Bells	Sheldon and Children
Falling Down (reprise)	Village Chorus
Let The River Flow	Geoffrey
Have Another Drink	Full Company
We'll Keep Running	Stranger and Alice
Letting Go	Abby, Mother and Company
I'll Be Here Waiting For You	Thomas, Catherine and Alice
Goodbye Children	Emily
If Only For The Children	Full Company

A Ring of Roses

ACT ONE

Prelude music is played as a single bell tolls and smoke covers the acting area. A low drone is heard. The Stranger approaches a cross downstage. He lays flowers by it, removes a silver cross hanging from it, stands and shouts - 'Why?' Villagers walk slowly into the dim light of the village and remain still whilst looking out towards the audience

A child's voice is heard singing off stage as the Stranger exits in darkness

> I've looked out of windows
> I've wished on the moon
> That someone out there loves me

Catherine steps forward and addresses the audience with musical vamp underneath. Children walk through the village and Villagers onto the hill area. Several parents either turn away or hold the children for the last time

Catherine It is 1665, the time of the Plague. A disease that spared no one. A disease that simply spread pain and suffering to all those that stood in its way.
The decision had been made to put the children onto the hill so as the Plague would not touch them. They were to be isolated from their village and from the people that loved them. It was not a time to die... just a time for letting go.

One of the Villagers enters into a separate part of the acting area and looks towards the children. They continue to walk through the gates and onto the hill. Abby turns and looks at the Villager. The Villager turns away and Abby continues to walk onto the hill with the others

Song

'THEY WILL BE, WHO THEY WILL BE'

Oh what have we done?
What will become of them?
A Ring of Roses lay where they once stood (Ring a Ring a Roses)
And day after day
Until they return again
We'll keep the fires burning as we should

Oh what have we done?
Why are we letting go?
What's the price we know they'll have to pay? (Ring a Ring a Roses)
And so out of reach
A place where they'll stand alone
Guide them through so they won't lose their way

And don't let them ask us why, don't let them see us cry
Left where the sun won't shine, we sold them the view from the hill

And they will be, who they will be
And they'll be strong, like we said to be
And they will sing, just like the dreamers holding dreams within their
hands
Such empty hands

(Repeat verse one with counter melody)

Oh what have we done? (Some day), What will become of them? (Some
one)
A Ring of Roses lay where they once stood (Will tell the story as it's
told)
And day after day (It's here), Until they return again (It's now)
We'll keep the fires burning as we should

And don't let them ask us why, don't let them see us cry
Left where the sun won't shine, we sold them the view from the hill

And they will be, who they will be
And they'll be strong, like we said to be
And they will sing, just like the dreamers holding dreams within their
hands...
...Such empty hands.

*During the song the Villagers could act out working in the village by
digging, stamping, chopping wood etc. More Villagers could enter during
the song holding lanterns and torches. The Children remain in the hill
area*

At the end of the song Abby's Mother rushes forward in the village area. She stares out towards the audience and then turns to the other Villagers

Mother We must stop them. We can't let them go onto the hill. Don't turn your back on them.

I Villager The decision's been made. The hill is the safest place for them, you know that.

Mother But they're our children. *(she grabs him)*

I Villager And whilst they're on the hill away from this village, the Plague will not touch them. Why don't you just go home.

Mother How can you say that!

2 Villager Look, we've all got children on that hill. You're not the only one who feels guilty. We had no choice.

Mother They're going to be so alone, so afraid. We were wrong to decide their fate.

3 Villager It was a decision we all made for the sake of the children. Yes, we may die but at least we have given them a chance to live.

Mother But what if we don't see them again. What if we never get to hold them that one last time?

3 Villager Look, as long as the Children don't come into contact with anyone who has the Plague and if they stay away from this village... they will live.

4 Villager We are farmers, we shall continue to work hard and think positively.

5 Villager We will provide them with fresh food.

6 Villager The village bell we will continue to ring for them.

I Villager And we will be strong like they will be strong.

The Villager puts his hand on the Mother's shoulder as she looks out towards the audience. The villagers turn and exit leaving the Mother standing alone

2 Villager *(turning back)* It will be alright... Abby will be fine. *(Villager exits)*

Mother *(to herself)* I hope so... I really do!

Abby stands during the song, as if standing on the hill. Abby's Mother closes the gates across the village area

Song

'WHERE ARE YOU NOW?'

A candle burns, for every moment
And as it fades, I will be gone
Each tide that turns, it turns unnoticed
And like the sea, you must be strong

Don't ask me why,
Oh don't say goodbye,
Just remember me and things I said

Where are you now? (We'll take the blame, we'll wait each day, we'll
wait forever)
Where are you now? (So far away, so all alone, we'll think of you)
Close your eyes, please realise
That wherever I'll be, I'll be thinking of you

Each tear that falls, it has a meaning
When wiped away, it means much more

Don't ask me why
Oh don't say goodbye
Just remember me and things I said

Where are you now? (We'll take the blame, we'll wait each day, we'll
wait forever)
Where are you now? (So far away, so all alone, we'll think of you)
A flower died, no one noticed her eyes
And wherever I'll be, I'll be thinking of you.

It is a summers day up on the hill. Peter (the bully) stands and makes a
sudden poetic speech. The other Children are keeping themselves busy
playing

Peter The summer sun. The lush green fields of England and Peter the Great
stands amongst the peasants ready to conquer whatever comes his way. It's
a time when you live for the hot afternoons, a time when sunsets last longer...
and there's no one to tell you what to do. *(he breathes in)* Just smell that...
Can you smell that?... Just breathe in and tell me what you smell... Well,
what do you smell?

Roland *(sniffing the air)* Sheep dung!

Peter Freedom... it's freedom you can smell!

Roland *(sniffs again)* No! It's definitely sheep dung.

Gilbert So what are you saying Peter?

Peter I'm saying, here we are, on our own with no one to answer to. We're
free... free to make our own decisions... free to do what we like.

Gilbert *(thinking)* So what are you saying Peter?!

Emily We're not free! We're isolated up here on the hill surrounded by this
thing called the Plague. We dunno what it looks like and we dunno what it
is... we just know it's out there.

Alice Yeah! Only a simpleton would believe we're free.

Roland *(putting his hand up)* I believe it!

They all look at him

Peter Oh just leave me alone the lot of you, especially you, you little squirt.

He takes the flower Emily has in her hand and throws it away. Gilbert and Roland are enjoying the conflict

Alice You purposely try and upset people don't you Peter? You haven't got a sensitive bone in your body.
Peter *(turns back)* You shouldn't have said that, especially not now I'm in charge... That's right... From now on you'll do what I say. I mean somebody's gotta make the decisions round here!
Alice And who said it was gonna be you?

He leans towards her and stares right into her face. The other Children are listening and watching closely

Peter Have you ever seen a dead person? A person who's riddled with the Plague. Suffering in agony with huge hard boils growing in their groin, with pussy swellings oozing all over the body... I didn't think so. Well I have! Edward Cooper, he died that way. One minute talking to Mrs Taymar in the street, the next minute... Dead! I heard the Plague had got him!

The children retreat frightened. Alice comforts them

Roland I'm really hungry now!
Emily You could be a boil couldn't you Roland.
Roland How d'ya mean?
Emily Ugly, hard and a real pain.
Roland Oh very funny.

Gilbert is laughing then stops when Roland looks at him

Geoffrey I think... I... I've got a b... boil. I've certainly got some sw... swellings.
Peter Yeah, it's called your head Geoffrey. *(raps him on the head with his knuckles)*
Geoffrey Pl... Plea... Please don't hit me Peter... Please Peter... don't, please!
Peter If I wanna hit you Geoffrey I will do, alright!
Alice Just leave him alone Peter.
Peter *(mimics her voice)* Just leave him alone Peter. I didn't mean anything by it. I was playing. *(he shouts at Geoffrey who is huddled up scared)* I was playing Geoffrey!!
Alice Just leave him alone.
Peter Oh yeah! And what are you gonna do about it?
Alice I said leave him alone.
Peter You're gonna get a slap one of these days, you wait.

Roland Girls... they get right up your nose don't they Peter.
Gilbert I've never had a girl up my nose!
Peter I've had enough of hanging around here, I'm off down to the stream...
anyone coming?

*Gilbert and Roland follow as Peter exits over the stile. Roland makes it
clear that he is second and Gilbert is third in charge. Catherine enters
as Emily approaches Geoffrey*

Emily Are you alright, Geoffrey?
Geoffrey I... th... think I might have... bra... brain damage.
Alice Oh don't say that Geoffrey, you'll end up looking like Gilbert.

Gilbert hears and turns around. Emily sees Abby sitting alone

Alice And where have you been Catherine?
Catherine Nowhere Alice, honest, I just went for a walk
Emily Alice! Look at Abby. Do you think she's okay.
Alice *(calls)* Abby! *(Abby looks at her)* Abby, come here, what's the matter?

Abby walks over and sits down

Abby Do you ever get scared Alice?
Alice Of course I do.
Emily We all get scared Abby.
Abby How come you never show it?
Alice With the likes of Peter around, it's best not to show any fear. You know
what he's like!
Emily So what are you scared of Abby?
Abby I'm scared that I'll never see my parents again.
Alice There's nothing wrong with having those kinds of feelings.

Goeffrey starts to cough

Geoffrey Do you think if someone's got a cough, they've got the Plague?

Everyone ignores him

Abby I just really miss them, especially my mother... it's going to be her
birthday soon. *(stands looking out to the audience)*
Emily You'll see her again Abby, don't worry.
Geoffrey I couldn't see for th... three hours once.
Alice *(standing)* You've got to stay strong... we've all got to stay strong to
survive.

The girls stand

Geoffrey I thought I had amnesia.
Alice *(turning)* Geoffrey, amnesia is when you forget.

The girls walk off

Geoffrey Bu... But I did forget! I forgot to open my eyes.

Scene change to inside the Hag's abode where three hags can be seen spitting and clearing their noses into a pot. This could be acted out on a cart representing the inside of their house. It could be pushed on by Dill and Lichen whilst Marjoram relaxes. Bottles of ointments, herbs and a pot can be seen

Marjoram The Sisters of Thyme.
Lichen Where? *(she looks around)*
Dill Here! We are the Sisters of Thyme.
Marjoram The Herbal Hags... Dill, Lichen and Marjoram. *(she pushes herself forward)*

They smile showing their black teeth

Dill Beautiful.
Lichen Charming.
Marjoram Witty.
Lichen Buxom...

They all look down at their chests and then towards the audience embarrassed

Well, three out of four ain't bad!

Dill and Magoram grab Lichen and push her head into the pot

Dill Well?
Lichen *(angrily)* Well what?
Marjoram Well, is it ready yet? *(she places her finger into the pot and tastes the contents)*
Lichen More spit needed!

They begin making horrific spitting sounds and nose snorting into the pot. This continues throughout the song

Song

'A LITTLE BIT OF SPIT'

Take a good look and believe that we are what you see
The sight of us might make you heave, but we'll kiss you for free
Is it so wrong to be nice for a price
While watching the ignorant die
Have a slice of pie

Ain't it a wonderful thing when the blind lead the blind
Finding a fresh pile of skin from their rotting behinds
Looks awful, smells awful, tastes awfully good
It's just what we're trying to make
It's a piece of cake

Oh just add a bit of spit, just a little bit and more
Add a little bit, just a little spit, little bit of spit and we'll be sure...
We've got the cure

Got to be vile for a while like the flea on the rat
Caring is just not our style, let us all drink to that
Cry on our shoulder, we'd rather you bleed
The flavour will then be so sweet
Drink it with some meat

(Vocal overlaps)

Oh just add a bit of spit, just a little bit and more
Add a little bit, just a little bit, little bit of spit and we'll be sure...
We've got the cure

(We won't ever drink a drop, not a single drop, no way
Never drink a drop, not a single drop, never drink a drop, you'll
hear us say...
We're here to stay)

Oh just add a little bit, just a little bit and more
Add a little bit, just a little bit, little bit of spit, and we'll be sure...
We've got the cure

Dill Sshh! Listen, can you hear the whispers?
Marjoram About John Newcombe. *(she thinks of him fondly)*
Lichen What, the most unpleasant man in the whole village?
Dill The biggest brute that ever breathed.

Marjoram sighs

Lichen The most repulsive specimen of man that ever lived.
Marjoram What about him? *(she is still in a dream)*

Dill He's dead!
Marjoram *(upset)* Oh!
Dill Is that all you can say, "Oh"?
Lichen Oh good.

They laugh

Dill Should have let a bit of blood.
Lichen Forty drops at least.
Dill An ounce or two of cordial jelop.
Lichen And a little bit of spit.

They spit. Lichen spits on Marjoram

Dill For the flavour!
Marjoram *(hopefully)* Would that have saved him?
Lichen No!! It would have killed him off quicker.

They laugh

Marjoram Herbs!
Lichen Now that would have saved him.
All Herbs!
Dill Some days I just can't explain it but it's like second sight, only... I can
  hear it in my head!
All Herbs!!!
Dill They shouldn't have cast us aside.
Marjoram They should've accepted us for what we are.
Lichen So let them crawl from their houses.
Marjoram Like rats from the straw.
Lichen Let them beg us for a cure.
Dill Sshh. Listen! Can you hear the sound... bang, bang, bang, bang.

She continues the sound underneath the dialogue

Lichen Hammer and nails. *(she joins in)*
Marjoram Boxes.
Dill For their bones.

They stop

Lichen There's gonna be bedlam in the village.

They laugh and the cart is pulled off

*The Chorus enter into the village, behind the village gates. The Children
can be seen in the hill area*

Song

'FALLING DOWN'

August 17th 1665,(Three dead)
August 21st 1665, (Six dead)
August 23rd 1665, Falling Down
August 24th 1665, (Two dead)
August 26th 1665, (Eight dead)
August 29th 1665, Falling Down

> Don't touch the children
> Please don't let them die
> See they're only children
> Left alone to cry

> (Give) Spare them all from this pain
> (Them) Side by side we will stand
> (One) Is tomorrow out of reach?
> (Day) Give us light, let them see

(Vocal split as the above is repeated with the following counter melody)

> For a moment, For a moment
> What's the price we have to pay to sleep at night, to take the day?
> For a moment, For a moment
> What's the price we have to pay to sleep at night, to take the day?

> Don't touch the children
> Please don't let them die
> See they're only children
> Left alone to cry

> (Give) Spare them all from this pain
> (Them) Side by side we will stand
> (One) Is tomorrow out of reach?
> (Day) Give us light, let them see... more

Letting go (Letting go) Letting go, it's the hardest thing to do
Letting go (Letting go) Letting go, it's the hardest thing to do.

Towards the end of the song, the gates are opened by Sheldon. At the end of the song, the Villagers turn and exit but several bodies remain lying on the cobbled street. They could wear masks to represent the fact that they are dying

Scene change to the Gravediggers in the village, Unwin and Jenkins. Unwin is struggling, pushing a cart full of tools. Jenkins is checking out the bodies for possessions and personal treasures to keep for himself. He kicks a couple of bodies to ensure that they are dead and chuckles to himself

Unwin *(shouting)* Bring out yer dead... bring out yer dead...
Jenkins Unwin, Unwin, Unwin. *(he stands, sniffs and scratches himself)*
Unwin *(looks around)* There's only one of me Jenkins!

Jenkins puts his arm around him

Jenkins How many times do I have to tell you about shouting, "Bring out yer dead"
Unwin But we're gravediggers, I thought that's what we're supposed to shout.
Jenkins Dead, half-dead, slightly maimed, a little peaky maybe... I couldn't care if they only had a touch of diarrhoea as long as we get to bury them.
Unwin ...Oh I see... and the more we bury, the more possessions we can take from 'em and keep for ourselves.
Jenkins You are learning quickly Unwin... you are learning very quickly indeed my boy. *(he finds a jacket he quite fancies off one of the bodies and tries it on for size)*
Unwin Oh that's nice!!

Song

'DIG ANOTHER HOLE'

I'd bury anything for a small fee
I'm not a greedy man, but I need the cash
I've made a little list of what they owe me
Gotta get my money but don't wanna get a rash
It's not an easy job for the queasy
A tiny little sneeze and then buried in a flash
Ain't that a shame!

It's only 'cos I care that I buries 'em
I'd shovel up their family for half the price
I'd even leave your legs sticking out when
A box will cost you double if you're not that nice
I'll rummage through the pickings that they leave me

I'd even take your teeth out and I wouldn't think twice
Ain't that a shame!

What a loverly bloke I am
I'd like to help them if I can
I'd share all I have with them
(spoken by Unwin: "Err, I think I get it!")
So I'll dig another hole.

I haven't got a house that I live in
To tell the honest truth, I've got nine or ten.
(counter melody sung by the dead bodies:
Dig us a hole now, please make it quick.
We now have nothing, ain't that a shame)
It's amazing what you soon acquire
I've got a pair of boots with the feet still in.
I always have a smile when I'm digging
When nobody is looking it becomes a grin
Ain't that a shame!

What a loverly bloke I am
I'd like to help them if I can
I'd share all I have with them
(spoken by Jenkins: "Get it?" *Unwin:* "Got it!" *Jenkins:* "Good!")
So we'll dig another hole. (Dig another hole, Dig another hole,
Dig another hole)

Unwin There is just one thing Jenkins.
Jenkins Oh yeah!
Unwin I'm not moaning about it or nothing, it's just that I always seem to be
the one doing all the hard work.

Jenkins lifts up the arm of one of the dead bodies

Jenkins You wanna hand? You ungrateful little so and so. I'll have you know
it was hard work for me yesterday when I had to bury old Osbourne. He
thought he had the Plague, then he got better.
Unwin Eh? Why did you bury him then?
Jenkins Well, he was just stepping off the cart, feeling much better, when I
accidentally ran him over. It took me four hours to bury him. Now that's
hard work!
Unwin Four hours?!
Jenkins Yeah, well he wouldn't lie still!
Unwin Oh he wasn't dead then?!
Jenkins Oh no! But you can't take any risks though, can you? Not nowadays!

Unwin Well that's all very well. You doing that for old Osbourne; but what have you ever done for me?

Jenkins *(hitting him round the head)* What have I ever...!! I gave you that shirt you're wearing. Belonged to Mr Hopkins that did. I even quite fancied it meself!

Unwin *(concerned)* Not the Mr Hopkins who got stabbed with a pitchfork and died? *(opens his jacket to reveal four bloodstained pitchfork holes in the shirt)*

Jenkins The very same. Look, let me just remind you of what your dear mum said just before I buried... before she popped her socks. Gawd bless her. *(he smiles and scratches himself)*

Unwin Actually Jenkins I always thought that was a bit strange my mother dying so suddenly. She was the healthiest woman in the whole village.

Jenkins Business wasn't good at the time you see Unwin... unlike now where they can't drop quick enough. *(he refers to the dead bodies laying around)*

Unwin Drop what quick enough?

Jenkins *(looks at him in disgust)* Anyway, just as I was shovelling in the last bit of dirt she said to me... *(deep voiced)* "Jenkins, look after young Unwin, cook him his meals..."

Unwin Is that what you call 'em... meals?

Jenkins Are you saying my cooking's tough?

Unwin Tough? It asked me for a fight twice! *(he turns away laughing)*

Jenkins doesn't look too pleased at Unwin laughing and mimes strangling him

Jenkins Just grab the other end of that body and wait for me to give the signal right? *(he grabs Unwin where it hurts!!)*

Unwin *(high voice)* Right!

Jenkins rushes over to one of the bodies leaving Unwin in pain

Jenkins Ready... one...

Unwin tries to lift his end of the body

No, not yet! *(he hits Unwin round the head)* You don't go on 'one'. Whoever heard of anyone going on 'one. That's your problem that is Unwin, you are too keen, too enthusiastic, always rushing. You're like a horse with the runs you are. Right, now after three... one, two, three...

Jenkins lifts his end of the body but Unwin has moved away thinking

Unwin We're close aren't we Jenkins?

Jenkins *(does not look happy)* Yeah, we're close... unfortunately.

Unwin Well, if I catch the Plague off any of these dead bodies I want you to bury me.

Jenkins *(he swiftly walks over to Unwin, resting his head on Unwin's shoulder)* Do you really mean that?

Unwin Yeah I do.

Jenkins *(smiles at the audience)* Well let me put your mind at rest young Unwin and tell you that from the heart of my bottom... to bury you would give me great pleasure. But until then, I've got a mouth like a camel's armpit and you've got an armpit like a camel's mouth. Time for a drink I'd say.

They both go to exit but Jenkins suddenly stops and turns to Unwin

Get the cart!

Unwin tries to lift the cart and suddenly notices the children on the hill by looking out towards the audience

Unwin Here Jenkins, look at those children on the hill. Are they the ones whose parents put them up there so as they wouldn't come into contact with the Plague?

Jenkins They're the ones! Smile and wave now Unwin 'cos I give 'em three days and then I reckon we'll be burying them.

Jenkins smiles and he and Unwin wave to the children then exit with the cart

The scene changes to the children on the hill who are also waving. Sheldon the mad boy also stands watching the gravediggers. He waves at them and then mimes digging graves and pulling the cart. He suddenly sees the other children watching him

Sheldon *(nervously)* Uh, oh! *(he notices Emily)* Phew! Hello lady.

Emily Hello Sheldon... have you got any news for me today?

Sheldon I might have. Have you got any pennies? I collects 'em see. *(he puts his hand out)*

Catherine What do you want with pennies? What is it you buy with them?

Sheldon I don't buy nothing. I throws them into the stream and watch them race towards the bridge. I like the ways they twist and shines in the water. *(he demonstrates what happens to the pennies)*

Emily You are a funny boy.

Sheldon The little ones always wins. Have you got any little ones? *(he wipes his sleeve across his nose)*

Catherine By the bridge you say? I often stand on the bridge, it's really quiet and peaceful down there isn't it?! *(she thinks of her meetings with Thomas)*

Sheldon *(to Catherine)* He's waiting for you he is. He always waits for you.
Catherine Who?
Sheldon He told me that you're the one who's as beautiful as a rose.
Catherine I'm sorry Alice. I've got to go and see him. I've got to go and see Thomas. He'll be waiting for me, I know he will.
Alice Catherine, No! Catherine!

Catherine exits over the stile

Sheldon But I see the roses on people's faces in little rings. Then the people die. I'm gonna be a gravedigger when I've grown big.
Geoffrey Have I got any roses on my face? I think I might have.
Sheldon *(looks at Geoffrey)* I don't like roses no more.
Emily What are you talking about now?
Sheldon I like you though lady, you're kind to me you are. You talks to me.

Emily gives him a kiss on the cheek

Abby Have you been near the village Sheldon?
Sheldon Might have! Have you got any pennies?
Alice If you have been near the village Sheldon, you shouldn't be up here. You know what our parents said. We shouldn't come into contact with anyone. That's why we're up here on the hill, so as the Plague can't get us.
Abby I'll give you a penny if you tell me what you've seen.
Sheldon I sees lots in the village. I sees 'em put the tailor man in a box and nail him in. In case he changes his mind I reckon! *(he laughs and pretends to nail the box)*
Emily How many graves are there now Sheldon?
Sheldon I dunno! Death won't get me 'cos it knows I'm too quick and I'll spit at it if it comes near. It's OK for me to come here though.
Abby How many? How many graves? *(she grabs Sheldon)*
Sheldon Uh! Oh! *(he covers his ears in fright)*
Emily Abby, stop it... you'll frighten him and he's the only source of information we've got. Sheldon have many villagers died?
Sheldon I don't know numbers. They confuses me. But I sees lots of people in the graveyard and lots of crying and not just in my head. With my own eyes. I laughs and dances to try and cheer them up, but they sends me away. They don't think it's funny putting a man in a hole. *(he dances around)*

The children watch and follow Sheldon. They exit

Geoffrey *(alone)* I didn't think it was funny when I saw Jones and Jenkins bury a woman head first with her feet sticking out of the ground. I hope I don't get buried like that!

The scene changes to Peter, Gilbert and Roland walking towards the bridge down by the stream. Peter is in front, the other two are strolling behind hitting things with sticks in their hands

Roland You'll get that Alice one day won't you Peter?
Peter I don't wanna talk about it. As my mum would say "there's none so blind as them what won't listen". *(he looks confused)*
Roland Clever your mum ain't she.

As Roland thinks about it, Gilbert pushes his way into second place behind Peter

Gilbert *(thinking)* So what are you saying Peter?
Peter I'm saying that sometimes people have got to be taught to listen. *(he pushes his fist into his hand)* They'll learn, you mark my words.

Roland pulls Gilbert back into third position

Gilbert So what are you saying Peter?
Peter I don't reckon we need girls anyway, I reckon we <u>just need food</u>.
Gilbert Well you know what they say.
Peter ...and what do they say Gilbert?
Gilbert "Come the man, come the moment" or is it "Come the moment, come the man"? I never understood it anyway.

They reach the bridge

Do you reckon this grass is a bit damp?
Peter Eh?
Gilbert Only, if it's damp I better not sit here. See, there's a long history of piles in my family. *(he sticks his bottom in the air)*
Roland That's made me come over all hungry again.
Peter Is that all you think about, your stomach?
Roland *(he thinks)* Yeah, well if I don't eat I'll end up shifting off this mortal curl wouldn't I!
Peter It's coil!
Roland Okay, this coil curl.
Gilbert There might be some fish in the stream that we could eat... there again what if the fish have got the Plague.

They continue to throw things into the stream

Roland *(standing)* Did you know that even the bread that Mrs Merrill usually leaves by the well has already been eaten.
Both Yeah, by you!
Roland *(sitting)* Well, I couldn't help it! Now if you ask me...

Peter Well we didn't ask you so shut up.
Gilbert I had an uncle who died of starvation once.
Peter Well he wouldn't have died twice would he.
Roland I'm still hungry!

Peter cups his hands as if catching something in the stream

Peter I think I've just found lunch for you Roland.
Roland What is it?
Peter It's a Dytiscus Pleurococcus
Gilbert *(interested)* Oh yeah!

Gilbert and Roland shrug at each other

Peter Careful, don't touch... it's watching.
Gilbert It's ugly!
Roland It's lunch!
Peter It lays its larva on its victim which then feeds off the blood. It may look harmless but it's deadly.

Peter shows it to Gilbert who backs off looking worried

Roland So, can I eat it Peter?

They look at him

I can't help it.
Peter You haven't got worms have you?
Gilbert If he had, he'd probably eat them as well.
Peter Why do I bother?

He looks to the heavens. Roland takes the Dytiscus Pleurococcus out of Peter's hands and puts it into his pocket. No one else notices

Catherine enters, she sees Peter, Roland and Gilbert

Catherine Oh, it's you lot.
Peter Well, well... lookie here... it's Miss Perfect. Don't tell me, Alice sent you down to find out what we're doing... No! I know why you're here. *(he tuts sarcastically)* You're gonna meet lover boy aren't you.
Gilbert Yeah! You're gonna meet lover boy. *(he thinks)* Who's lover boy, Peter?
Peter Thomas Cobb.
Roland But I thought no one from the village was allowed up here.
Catherine Just stay out of this Peter. You say anything and I'll...
Peter You'll what?

Catherine I'll tell everybody about how you cried when you accidentally got locked in my father's barn 'cos you were scared of the dark.
Roland *(laughing)* Ha! Did you Peter? Did you cry because of the dark?

Peter grabs Roland and stares at him

Oops sorry Peter!
Peter *(lying)* Well for your information, Thomas was here just as we arrived.
Gilbert Was he?

Peter hits him

Peter And he said he didn't want to see you anymore. He was fed up with waiting and he'd rather spend time with his sheep.
Roland I like sheep!
Catherine You're lying Peter, Thomas didn't say that.
Peter Well do you see him here now? I think not and I bet you were due to meet him here as well weren't you. Ahh!! What a shame.
Catherine I hate you Peter.
Peter Come on boys, it's beginning to smell around here.
Roland *(sniffing the air)* Is it sheep dung again? Here, I wonder if sheep dung is eatable?!
Peter It's edible.
Roland Is it? Oh great! We might find some on the way back.

The boys exit leaving Catherine standing on the bridge alone

Catherine Oh Thomas I'm sorry. I promised I would meet you and I meant it. I didn't mean to be late. You wouldn't say that you don't want to meet me anymore! You wouldn't say that to Peter would you? Oh Thomas! Now what am I to do?

Song

'TRY'

Like a sparkle in the rain
Like a wave upon the shore
These are things I know that you'll remember
Like a kiss upon the cheek
And a gentle smile I'm sure
bring a brighter day for us

So Try
Please won't you close your eyes and try to see
The things you want to see
Don't cry

Look deep inside, I know they still believe, the way we still
believe
In you

Like a Summers eve in June
Like a wish upon the Moon
These are things I know that you'll remember
Like a feeling deep inside
And the pain you're trying to hide
You'll see they're not so far away

So Try
Please won't you close your eyes and try to see
The things you want to see
Don't cry
Look deep inside, I know they still believe, the way we still
believe
In you

A brighter day will come and soon we'll see the sun fall no more
Don't try to shut us out, to leave a sense of doubt, what's it for?

So Try
Please won't you close your eyes and try to see
The things you want to see
Don't cry
Look deep inside, I know they still believe, the way we still
believe
In you

During the song the Children enter into a neutral acting area carrying candles

Thomas arrives towards the end of the song and stands watching her. He walks up behind her and puts his hands over her eyes

Thomas Guess who?!

Catherine Oh Thomas! *(she throws her arms around him)* I thought you didn't want to see me ever again.

Thomas No, you silly girl. I told Sheldon to pass the message on to you but I was nearly seen by the gravediggers so I had to come the long way round. I'm just a bit late that's all.

Catherine looks at him, then looks away

Catherine How's everything in the village? How are my parents?

He steps away

Thomas You can't see the disease, it just eats away at people. So many have died Catherine. I've never seen anything like it, bodies everywhere waiting to be buried and yet the villagers carry on as if nothing's happening. *(he looks at her)* Don't worry Catherine your parents are fine.

Catherine It's horrible Thomas, just waiting everyday not knowing what's going to happen. Not knowing whether the people you love are alive or dead. If you hadn't turned up today I don't know what I would have thought.

Thomas And that's why I've got it all worked out. *(he grabs her hands)*

Catherine I don't understand!

Thomas No more secret meetings, or hoping that the other person will still be alive. No more sneaking around behind people's backs.

Catherine What are you saying?

Thomas Come away with me. Look, within the last three days, Mrs Cooper has buried her husband and two members of her family. She fled to another village this morning, one that hasn't been touched. It's the obvious thing to do!

Catherine What? You want me to run away with you?

Thomas I've thought it all through. There's nothing here for us. This is a time for adventure... it's not a time to die and that's exactly what is going to happen if we don't run away now.

Catherine turns away

Catherine, listen to me.

Catherine Don't confuse me Thomas. I can't just leave. What about the others? They need me. *(she turns away)*

Thomas Don't play games with me Catherine.

Catherine I'm not going anywhere with you Thomas. You've got no right to decide what I want.

Thomas *(pause)* But I thought you loved me!

Catherine I do! But it's too soon to make such a decision.

Thomas Look I'll meet you here in two days. Maybe you would have changed your mind by then. It will at least give you time to think. *(he goes to leave)*

Catherine Thomas...

He turns

...be careful.

They embrace

Song

'I'LL BE HERE WAITING FOR YOU (Preview)'

In my life, I've never seen
One like her who touches me
No one knows how good it's been
Once upon a Summers dream

A girl whose face is smiling
A girl whose love I've found
My world is turning around
But I'll be here waiting for you

Scene change to the children back on the hill. Sheldon has noticed Peter, Roland and Gilbert entering. Roland has sheep dung around his mouth

Sheldon Uh oh! Nasty man. I gotta goes and finds some pennies.

Peter enters with Roland and Gilbert

Peter Well, well, well, if it's not the mad boy.
Emily His name is Sheldon.
Peter I don't care what his name is. I just know he's a freak.
Emily He's not a freak.
Peter You been telling them your stories have you freak?
Sheldon They're not stories, they're things I sees.
Peter You answer me back again freak and you'll see the back of my hand.
Emily Oh, that's very big of you Peter.

He goes to hit her but stops

Sheldon I don't like you mister.
Peter Oh, I'm heart-broken.
Sheldon I hope your bones get polished and hung out in the sun to dry.

Peter grabs Sheldon by the throat with one hand

Peter Have you ever seen a boy hang? His face goes purple and his eyes pop! It can be arranged... little weasel.

Sheldon exits

Emily Why do you have to torment him? He hasn't done anything to you.
Peter Oh shut up Miss Goody, Goody.
Emily Why don't you crawl in a hole Peter? *(she exits after Sheldon)*
Peter I can't find one big enough. *(he smiles sarcastically)*
Geoffrey I... I got pushed d... down a hole once.

Peter You can shut up as well Geoffrey, no one wants to hear about your sob stories, your make believe illnesses, or the things that have occurred in your pathetic little life.

Geoffrey B... but I had to stay down there f... for two days. He said I n... n... needed to be punished.

Abby Who did Geoffrey?

Geoffrey My f... fath...

Peter Oh don't humour him, just go away.

Gilbert and Roland go to walk off

Not you two! Geoffrey... I was talking to Geoffrey! Go on Geoffrey hop it and give us all a break.

Geoffrey moves to another part of the acting area

Alice *(to Peter)* What did you do that for?

Peter Why? Have you got a problem with it?

Alice You're full of it aren't you? You tell people what to do and they do it, you humiliate people and they take it. You're asking for it you are. *(she pushes him)*

Peter Oh yeah, and who's gonna give it to me then. *(he looks around and then grabs Alice's face)* I don't think you quite grasp the situation. I'm the biggest and I'm in charge. *(he throws her to the floor and then walks off to lie in the sun)*

Gilbert Roland, what have you got round your mouth?

Roland Nothing!

Gilbert 'Cos it don't half look and smell like sheep dung.

Roland walks off embarrassed, Gilbert follows apologetically

Abby *(to Alice)* That was very brave of you Alice, standing up to Peter like that.

Roland I stood up for myself once. It was when I was working in my father's field. I told 'em it was my field and that they had no right to be on it. They didn't take too kindly to my views and after several heated words they moved on. I think it was because I told them to 'Get lost!'

Gilbert Roland, they were sheep.

Roland Yeah, but it proved who was in charge!

Emily re-enters but without Sheldon

Gilbert You was a bit like that Dytiscus Pleurococcus then, just waiting for the right time to strike. *(pause)* Where is the Dytiscus Pleurococcus anyway? I didn't see you put it back in the stream!

Roland looks guilty

Roland I ate it!

Gilbert points to Roland's stomach

Gilbert So it's in there?! *(he prods and listens to Roland's stomach)*
Roland I couldn't help it. Apparently they hate rejection I felt sorry for it.
Emily So you ate it to make it feel good?

Roland nods

A Dytiscus Pleurococcus?

Roland nods again

You are one sick individual Roland.
Roland I think I might be soon... I don't feel too good.
Gilbert You don't think you've got the big 'P' do you?
Roland No, I had one of those over by the tree this morning.
Abby He means the Plague.
Emily He looks fine to me.
Roland How do you know what I should look like if I've got this Plague?
Emily Sheldon told me... sometimes you get little marks on your face like
roses, which then develop into black boils all over your body and other
times the person just smells a sweet scent in the air and they die a peaceful
death.
Roland Is anyone else peckish or is it just me?
Gilbert There you go again.

The Hags enter into a different acting area collecting herbs

Song

'WHERE'S MY DINNER?'

Where's my dinner?
I haven't eaten for a week, I've sort of gone off sheep
Grass is very good
I'd rather have some Bread Pud, yes I would
Call yourself a mate, I haven't got a plate
And even if I had
(Counter melody: Yum, Yum, Yum, Yum, Yum etc etc)
Where's my supper.
I haven't eaten much for lunch, I need something to munch
Rabbit stew is nice

I'd rather have some blind mice, for a price
Call yourself a friend, I'm going round the bend
Just a little slice

Serve it up
Lumpy or smooth
It will go down
Serve it up
It's all that we ask right now
(repeat verse one with the following two counter melodies:

Children: Yum, Yum, Yum, Yum, Yum, Yum, Yum

Hags: Rosemary and Thyme, Fenugreek and Tarragon
Coriander doesn't rhyme, add a little sage and
Rosemary and Thyme, Fenugreek and Tarragon
Coriander doesn't rhyme

Where's my dinner?

At the end of the song Catherine enters

Catherine *(to Peter)* I hate you Peter Hawkes. You're a liar and I hate you.

Peter waves. Gilbert and Roland copy him. Catherine walks over to Alice

I'm sorry I ran off Alice. I just had to see him. Please don't be angry with me.
Alice Catherine we were told not to speak to anyone who wasn't already on the hill and yet you stupidly go and have a meeting with Thomas. I take it, it was Thomas?!
Catherine But I love him Alice and he loves me!
Alice And once this is all over, you'll be able to see him as much as you like.
Catherine If he survives!

They look at each other

So many have died in the village already Alice.
Alice He'll survive.
Catherine *(turns away)* He also wants me to run away with him.
Alice Oh no Catherine... you wouldn't?!

Scene change to village where the villagers continue to work hard. They suddenly see Thomas return through the gates to the village. He is singing, 'A girl whose face is smiling...'

Villager You're in a good mood Thomas. Where have you been?

Thomas doesn't reply

Villager Well, answer us boy!
Thomas I... er...
Villager Leave the poor lad alone, look you're scaring him.
Villager We asked you a question Thomas, where have you been?

Thomas is grabbed

Thomas I can't say.
Villager Leave him be.

Sheldon appears through the crowd

Sheldon He's been on the hill he has. *(he is pleased with himself)*
Villager How do you know boy?
Sheldon They be things I sees mister, with my own eyes.
Villager Thomas, is this true?
Mother Did you see the children, Thomas?
Villager *(angrily)* Stay out of this.
Mother What about Abby, Did you see her, is she alright?
Villager I said stay out of this.

The Mother is pushed away as they crowd around Thomas

Sheldon I would see more if I had some pennies mister. *(he puts his hand out but gets a clip round the ear)*
Villager Why do it Thomas? Why put yourself and those children at risk?
Thomas I just needed to make sure that Catherine...
Villager *(shocked)* Catherine! You did this for Catherine!? Ignorance is for fools, Thomas!
Mother I told you it was wrong to put those children onto the hill. I told you all and yet none of you would listen to me!
Villager Can you not see what has happened? Can you not see what Thomas has done?
Thomas I wasn't thinking... I'm sorry!
Villager You disobey us and you're sorry!
Thomas I was scared, I just wanted to make sure Catherine was still alive.

Thomas get pushed to the ground

Villager We're all scared Thomas. We're all living from day to day in the hope that one morning we will wake up and the nightmare will be gone.
Mother Leave him alone.

Villager Don't you ever disobey us again boy.

Thomas ...I won't... I won't leave the village again... I promise.

Villager We agreed to work hard in this village to ensure that there would be a place for our children to return to.

Villager If you have passed the Plague on.

Thomas is grabbed and lifted up

Thomas But I haven't got the Plague.

Villager If you've put those children's lives in danger, it won't be the Plague that brings your life to an end. *(he throws Thomas upstage)*

Hags have already entered on their cart

Song

'SEE THIS PLAGUE'

See these hands, see how they...
See these eyes, see what they've...
See how we...
See how we...
See how it twists and it turns as it passes and casts you the blame

> She'll ask you to beg as she strips you of pride
> With one kiss and one touch, see them run, see them hide
> And sooner or later, another one dies

Intro

> See these hands, see how they...
> See these eyes, see what they've...
> See how we...
> See how we...
> See how it twists and it turns as it passes and casts you the blame

> She'll ask you to beg as she strips you of pride
> With one kiss and one touch, see them run, see them hide
> And sooner or later, another one dies

Hags: Oh it's so pure and simple
Oh it's so beautifully obvious
Oh as tame as the Moon in your hand, she will hold you
La, la, la, la, la, la, la
La, la, la, la, la, la, la

She'll ask you to beg as she strips you of pride
With one kiss and one touch, see them run, see them hide
And sooner or later, another one dies

This song could involve choreographed stomping and the use of sticks as if working in the village..

Scene change to Hags. The Villagers exit

Lichen From the cradle to the grave.
Dill A few more dead.
Lichen and **Dill** Clunk!! *(they drop their heads)*
Lichen Not quite the number we had hoped. *(she looks at Marjoram spitefully)*
Dill No matter!
Lichen It still decreases the population.
Dill Let them die.
Marjoram And leave the good looking men to me.

Lichen and Dill look at her

Lichen For have they asked for our help yet?
All They have not.

They spit, again Lichen spits on Marjoram who feels it

All From the cradle to the grave.
Marjoram Boils.
Lichen Headaches.
Dill Fever.
Lichen A small cough.

Dill coughs

Marjoram A strange sweet smell.

They sniff the air

All A ring of roses.
Lichen Roses without thorns.
Dill Roses in summer.

They all look towards the hill area

All The children.
Marjoram We owe it to the children.

Lichen They should not suffer.
Dill Much.
Marjoram They need herbs.
Lichen Herbs to heal.
Marjoram A Plague to kill.
Dill More spit needed.

They spit into the pot. This time Majoram watches Lichen who innocently spits into the pot. Dill suddenly gasps

Lichen *(impatient)* What is it now?
Dill I see a stranger.
Marjoram The Plague?
Dill A man?
Lichen And is he... *(she sighs)* ...handsome?
Marjoram If he is, he's mine.
Dill The children.
Marjoram Forget the children.
Lichen Tell us about the stranger.
Marjoram Is he well formed?
Lichen Is he well endowed?

They look at her

Dill He's heading for the children.

They rub their hands together

Marjoram *(sighs)* Ohh! May he push them aside and come to us!
All When shall we three eat again!

The cart is pulled off

Scene change back to village. Abby's mother approaches Thomas who is staring out to the audience as if looking out to the hill

Mother Thomas. Did you see Abby?
Thomas No... ma'am, I didn't.
Mother Did Catherine say how she was?
Thomas She didn't say anything I'm sorry! I'm sure she's fine.
Mother I hope you're right, I really do!

A light comes up on Catherine and as she delivers the speech, the children stand behind her and stare out towards the audience

Catherine It was a strange evening with a touch of warmth in the air that was cooling fast under a rosy sunset. Being amongst the trees up on a hill made you forget about the disease. It was a time for friendships and adventure... and as Thomas had said "it was not a time to die".

The children settle down to sleep. Villagers join Abby's Mother in the village. They carry lanterns.

During the song Abby stands and sings the counter melody, "Mama I Miss you, How do I Miss you"

Song

'GOODNIGHT CHILDREN'

When day has turned to night, close your eyes
And then things will be alright, find the light
But don't ask me how I feel inside
I won't know what to say

You don't know what you've got, till it's gone
And I promised you the world, I was wrong
So don't ask me how I feel inside
I've never felt so cold

So Goodnight Children
Let the dreamers sleep
As still as a boat at sea
So rest now children
Summer days to keep
And sleep for a chance to dream

How many times must we close our eyes
To learn how to understand, realise
But don't ask me how I feel inside
I wish that you were here

So Goodnight Children
Let the dreamers sleep
As still as a boat at sea
So rest now children
Summer days to keep
And sleep for a chance to dream

Abby Night Mama... I love you.

The villagers exit as the children sleep. A stranger appears under the moonlight. A drone can be heard as the bell tolls. He looks around and smiles as the drone gets louder. As the lights fade the drone stops. The Stranger puts his arms out to form the shape of a silhouetted cross.

END OF ACT ONE

ACT TWO

*A single bell tolls as smoke covers the acting area. The company make
their way to different parts of the stage holding candles and lanterns
as if in prayer or mourning*

Song

'LET THEM CRY'

See how the candle burns
See how the sun did shine
We will still think about them
See how they run

Give them a guiding light (Give them the light)
Give them the warmth they need (Give them the warmth)
Show them the view from the hill (Show them the view)
See how they smile

    And if they live
    And if we die
    Let them cry
    All they want to cry

    And if they ask
    And wonder why
    Let them cry
    All they want to cry

No one to say goodnight
No one to hold them tight
Will they still think about us
Where are they now?

Don't let the Winter come (Give them the light)
Don't let the end be near (Give them the warmth)
Hold on to what you have got (Show them the view)
Don't be afraid

    And if they live
    And if we die
    Let them cry
    All they want to cry

And if they ask
And wonder why
Let them cry
All they want to cry

All exit after song. Change of scene to Unwin entering with his cart.
Jenkins follows behind

Unwin *(shouting)* Bring out your dead, half dead, slightly maimed...
Jenkins *(shouting)* Unwin?
Unwin Yes Jenkins.
Jenkins Shut up!
Unwin Yes Jenkins.
Jenkins Thank you!

Sheldon appears. Unwin sees him

Unwin Hello boy!
Sheldon Hello Mr Jones... hang on! You're not Jones, who is ya?
Jenkins His name's Unwin.

Sheldon spits on his hand and holds it out for Unwin to shake. Unwin
obliges and then wishes he hadn't

Sheldon Hello Nunwin. I wanna be a gravedigger, where's your shovels?
Unwin We haven't started digging yet boy. And my name's Unwin not Nunwin.
Sheldon Yeah alright Nunwin, keep your hair on!
Jenkins Oi! Have you finished yacking? 'Cos we got work to do. *(to Sheldon)*
Now go away you 'orrible little bag of bones before I put my foot down with
a firm hand!
Sheldon *(to Jenkins)* You ain't got no manners you ain't mister. *(to Unwin)*
Have you got any farthings Nunwin? I can't get any pennies, people says they
ain't got no more.
Jenkins *(shocked)* We haven't got any money and even if we had, we wouldn't
give any to you, so bugger off!
Sheldon Bad fings are gonna happen to you, you had better watch out you
had.

Sheldon goes off to study the tools on the cart. He particularly likes the
shovel and decides to dance with it, holding it close

Jenkins Bad fings have already happened to me... I ended up with you two!
(he smiles a sarcastic smile)
Unwin Here Jenkins, what did happen to Jones, the apprentice gravedigger
what you had before me?
Jenkins I buried him. *(they look at him)* Well, he did ask me to!

Unwin You don't intend burying me just yet do you Jenkins? I pacifically remember mentioning that I'd like you to bury me <u>when I'm dead</u>.

Jenkins I'd bury anything for a small fee, dead or alive. *(he looks at Sheldon and smiles)*

Unwin But Jones only had a stomach ache.

Jenkins Well, beggars can't be choosers young Unwin, that's something you gotta learn that is, now that you're my new apprentice.

Sheldon walks up to Unwin whilst still holding the shovel

Sheldon So, what are we doing now then Nunwin?

Unwin snatches the shovel off Sheldon

Unwin I'm gonna have a rest, if I may!

He looks at Jenkins who looks at him in disgust. Unwin sits on the cart

Sheldon *(to Jenkins)* I've seen you and Nunwin dragging those bundles of washing. I always like the way the legs stick out. That's funny that is.

Jenkins We gotta bury the dead somehow boy without touching them.

Unwin *(angrily)* And it's Unwin, not Nunwin.

Sheldon Sshh. *(he can hear the village bells ringing)* They be my friends, they be Mister.

Unwin walks over listening to the bells

Jenkins They're bells you silly little twerp!

He hits Sheldon round the head. Unwin copies him

Children enter the acting area representing the bells

Song

'STILL HEAR THE SOUND OF THE BELLS'

Hey you, can you hears what I can hears?
Ding Dong, the sound of the bells that is
We've been the bestest of friends for years
That be the sound of the bells

Hear that, each bell tells a diff'rent tale
Four chimes, a sound I remembers well
Secrets, I know I must never tell
All from the sound of the bells

Giants do tremble and hide away
Beggars and Choosers and Kings hear no words
Time waits for no one that's what they say
Ding Dong (Ding Dong) Ding Ding Dong (Ding Ding Dong)
Wherever I go... I still hears the sound of the bells

See how all the rats run away
Easy come, Easy go they say
I'll sit listening all the day
List'ning to sounds of the bells

And if the bells stop I'll remember them
A ring far sweeter than any a Rose
And if all at once I'm without a friend
Ding Dong (Ding Dong) Ding Ding Dong (Ding Ding Dong)
Wherever I go... I still hears the sound of the bells

Ding Dong... Ding Dong Ding Dong... Ding Ding a Ding Dong... etc etc

And if the bells stop I'll remember them
A ring far sweeter than any a Rose
And if all at once I'm without a friend
Ding Dong (Ding Dong) Ding Ding Dong (Ding Ding Dong)
Wherever I go... I still hears the sound of the bells

During the song Jenkins tries to measure Sheldon but ends up getting frustrated with Unwin who is only interested in what Sheldon is singing about

Jenkins How tall are you boy?
Sheldon I've been watching the ants Nunwin... *(he is oblivious)*
Unwin My name's Unwin NOT Nunwin.
Sheldon ...They was all in a line, following each other into a hole...
Jenkins You gotta show 'im who's in charge Unwin!
Sheldon ...helping each other out they was...
Unwin I've gone right off children anyway.
Sheldon ...so I kicked it all up to see what was inside...
Jenkins Good point! Those children on the hill should have popped their socks by now.
Sheldon ...and they ran all over the place...
Unwin They should have snuffed it by now as well!
Jenkins *(looks at him)* Do you reckon that last hole we dug would be big enough for all of them? *(he measures them from a distance)*
Sheldon ...so I trod on them and they all cried.
Unwin Ants don't make noises boy.
Sheldon *(whispers)* It was quiet crying Nunwin... quiet crying.

Jenkins Oi oi, who's that up on the hill? If it's a child he ain't half grown.

Music drone begins as the stranger appears on the hill

Sheldon Uh oh, that's no child, that's a man... or it could be the Plague come to get the children.
Jenkins Gonna have to make that hole much bigger now... *(he looks at Sheldon)* Do you get frightened boy?
Sheldon Only of those giants that's in the sky and the grumbles they make. *(he puts his hands over his ears)*
Jenkins Good, then go and find a shovel for yourself and help us dig. We're gonna need a big hole I reckon.
Sheldon Oh thanks Mister Jenkins. *(he spits on his hand and shakes Jenkins's hand)* Thanks Nunwin.

Sheldon then jumps up and kisses Unwin on the cheek. Unwin just stares at the audience

Unwin *(depressed)* It's Unwin... not Nunwin.

A light comes up on the villagers desperate in the village. The gravediggers exit during the song with Sheldon riding on the cart

Song

'FALLING DOWN' (reprise)

Stranger on the hill, standing all alone (Look there)
Running out of time, children on their own (So scared)
Nothing we can do, will they ever know? (Falling Down)

Stranger on the hill, does he really care? (So near)
Take a look around, is he running scared? (No fear)
Tell us what to do, 'cos there's no one there (Falling Down)

      Don't touch the children
      Please don't let them die
      See they're only children
      Left alone to cry

(Give) Spare them all from this pain
(Them) Side by side, we will stand
(One) Is tomorrow out of reach?
(Day) Give us light, let them see
...Stranger on the hill

The Villagers point out towards the audience on the last note

Scene change to Peter walking to the bridge. Geoffrey is already sitting staring into the water. Peter sees Geoffrey and goes to sit next to him. Geoffrey thinks Peter is going to hit him and covers his head to protect himself

Geoffrey *(shying away)* Ple... please don't hit me again P... Peter. Pl... please don't!

Peter I'm not gonna hit you Geoffrey. What are you doing down here on your own anyhow? *(he sits down)*

Geoffrey *(still nervous)* N... nothing Peter, honest!

Peter You're not suffering from one of your fake illnesses again are you?

Geoffrey I just come here to be on my own and th... they're not f... fake illnesses.

Peter Yes they are Geoffrey, they're all in your head.

Geoffrey I might have an illness.

Peter I reckon you just miss your parents.

Geoffrey No I don't! I don't miss 'em at all.

Peter You must do... everyone misses their parents!

Geooffrey I... I... haven't got any! *(he turns his head away)*

Peter Yes you have... I seen you with your father.

Geoffrey *(looks scared)* The only thing I miss is going to church.

Peter *(standing)* What is the matter with you Geoffrey? I can't work you out. I mean, being out here is a symbol of manhood, a chance to prove yourself. It's a bit like when my father was given a job loading barrels onto the village cart. For his initiation they covered him in malt, shut him in a barrel and rolled him down the biggest hill they could find. OK, he was so badly injured that he never got to prove himself as a barrel loader, but it proved he was a man... you don't talk about your father much do you?

Geoffrey *(turns away)* He used to beat me that's why!

Peter No!... you're having me on.

Geoffrey lifts up his shirt and reveals bruise marks and cuts

Peter Blimey! What did you do for him to beat you?

Geoffrey Nothing! He'd get drunk or have a bad day at work and come in and hit us until it made him feel better. He would hit our poor mother as well... she left just after my brother James died. I woke up one morning and she had gone. I wish she had taken me! *(he bows his head)*

Peter I didn't know you had a brother.

Geoffrey He was only trying to protect me Peter, but instead he got hit round the head with a barn fork used to rake up the hay. They said he died immediately.

Peter At least up here you're away from your father.

Geoffrey *(looks up, his face showing tearful anger)* With any luck the Plague would have got him and given him what he deserves.

Peter Oh no, don't talk like that Geoffrey.

Geoffrey You don't know what it's like Peter. I've got pictures in my head that will never go away. Oh yeah, the bruises will, but the nightmares won't.

Peter I'm sorry... I really am. *(he sits)*

Geoffrey *(pause)* I still think of him Peter, James that is... my brother... I do miss him.

Song

'LET THE RIVER FLOW'

No matter what we do, everything we say
Always will remain with me
I cannot change the past, things don't always last
Please will you remember me

> Wherever you may be now
> Wherever you may be
> You'll live to tell, live to tell, it well

And when you stand alone, I'll be there for you
Never will I leave your side
Take each day as it comes, through the fields we'll run
Lift your head and don't you cry

> Wherever you may be now
> Wherever you may be
> You'll live to tell, live to tell, it well

Let the river flow
Let it join on to the sea, where I know you'll be
Let the water fall
'Till it has no where to go, let the river flow
Let the river flow

No matter what we do, everything we say
Always will remain with me
I cannot change the past, things don't always last
Please will you remember me

> Wherever you may be now
> Wherever you may be
> You'll live to tell, live to tell, it well

Let the river flow
Let it join on to the sea, where I know you'll be
Let the water fall
'Till it has no where to go, let the river flow
Let the river flow

Peter Here, what about if you were to stay with us.
Geoffrey Eh?
Peter My mother would look after you... and well, you could be my brother.
It'd mean me fighting you every now and then though!

Geoffrey smiles and Peter puts his arm around him

*A light comes up on the Hags who are standing outside the village
gates*

All *(whispering)* Children of winter, Children of winter... *(continued)*
Marjoram Children of Winter.
Lichen Children of Winter.
Dill Children of Winter. Bow'd low.
Lichen *(echoes)* Children of Winter. Bow'd low.
Marjoram Gone is the summer.
Lichen Sunshine and laughter.
Dill All that is left.
All Grief and woe.

They smile, open the gates and enter the village

*Scene change back to children on the hill. Emily is standing looking out
towards the audience*

The Stranger is watching. He is eating an apple

Catherine What are you looking at Emily?
Emily I was just watching Sheldon helping the gravediggers dig more graves.
It's funny, but being up here you forget about your worries and the reason
why you're up here.
Catherine You've always got time for Sheldon haven't you? You obviously
like him.
Emily I feel sorry for him. He's got no one has he? No one to care for and
no one who cares for him.
Catherine He's got you.
Emily Supposing you die and nobody misses you. You live and you die and
the difference doesn't affect a single person in the whole world.
Catherine Sheldon won't die.

Alice has seen him, but stands motionless

Emily It's as if you had never existed in the first place.

Catherine Emily, we can't be touched up here - you said so yourself. Can't you think of better things and anyway, remember what the Vicar said, "Though shalt not be afraid of the terror by night, for a thousand shall fall at thy side..."

Stranger "...and ten thousand at thy right hand, but it shall not come near thee." It's a wise thing to remember young lady.

They all turn and stare towards the Stranger. He is wearing a large silver cross around his neck. The same cross he was holding in the opening scene

Emily Who are you?

Stranger Good question... who are any of us?! *(he throws his bag down and takes off his hat)*

Gilbert It's the Plague, he's come to get us. It is... it's the Plague.

Stranger *(arrogant)* Could be!

They back off in terror

Roland *(falling to his knees)* Please don't kill me... I'm really sorry that I locked those sheep in the church... it was Gilbert's idea!!

Gilbert No it wasn't!

Roland It was. I wouldn't do such a thing! *(he tries to make out he is an 'angel')*

Alice He's not the Plague. *(she stares at him)*

Gilbert How do you know? You don't know what the Plague looks like. No one does!

Catherine *(to Stranger)* You shouldn't be up here.

Stranger *(nastily)* Am I not welcome then?

Emily Who are you?

Stranger *(he bows to Emily)* I'll be whoever you want me to be.

The children look on as he juggles three apples that he has pulled from his bag. He throws the apples to the children

Catherine *(to the children)* Don't touch them... I said don't touch them and don't go near him. *(she pulls the children away)*

Child But it's food Catherine - we need as much food as we can get hold of.

Stranger Children alone on a hill eh? That's brave!

Catherine Look Mister, I think you had better go, before you scare the children. *(she holds them close to her)*

Stranger *(angrily)* I'm just passing through. There's no law against it is there?

Alice Where have you come from then?
Catherine Alice!
Alice No, I want to know!

The Stranger stares at her but says nothing

Why are you looking at me like that?

The Stranger's tone of voice changes as he looks towards Alice

Stranger *(softly)* Her freckles used to come out in the sun just like yours.

Alice gets embarrassed

Oh I'm sorry...! I didn't mean to...
Emily Who are you talking about Mister?
Child And why do you stare at Alice like that?

The Stranger suddenly snaps out of his trance of thought

Child I want to know where he comes from!

The children watch him cautiously

Stranger London, that's where I come from. London! A place riddled with
vermin and disease. Not for your eyes that's for sure. *(he looks towards
Alice again)* You remind me so much of her. *(he goes to touch Alice's
face)*
Catherine No! Don't you dare.
Alice Who do I remind you of Mister? You're not making any sense.
Gilbert I went to London once and saw the King on his horse.
Roland What was it like?
Gilbert Four legs... a tail...
Roland No!! What was it like going to London to see the King?
Child I'm gonna see the King one day and tell him how brave we were to be
up here.
Child My father will take me.

The stranger is not well and keeps clutching his side and coughing

Stranger So, where are your parents then?
Abby They're down there in the village. They made the decision to put us up
here on the hill so as we would survive, even if... even if they die. *(she
bows her head)*
Stranger So they're down there, just waiting for the day when they can see
you again? That's madness!

Roland I reckon they're down there getting drunk. That's what they usually
did in the evenings.
Gilbert Yeah... I can see it now. *(staggers about and hiccups, acting drunk)*

A light comes up on the villagers who are drunk. The children join in

Song

'HAVE ANOTHER DRINK'

We haven't had a sleep for a week now
We would have said it's worry, but we know it's drink
It's difficult to know how to speak when
We have to make decisions but we can't quite think
No matter what we feel deep inside now
The drunk are getting drunker and we're on the brink
Ain't that a shame

We tried our very best to be good but
The wine it tastes of water and was rather nice
We even chased the sheep for a laugh
And we'd do it all again so we wouldn't think twice
But if we had to kiss all the hags
Then we'd only ever do it for a bloomin' good price
Ain't that a shame

We're only drinking 'cos there's nothing left
And if we didn't we'd be so depressed
The only thing is now we've got bad breath
(spoken by Gilbert, 'But who cares?')
So we'll have another drink

We haven't had a sleep for a week now
We would have said it's worry, but we know it's drink
It's difficult to know how to speak when
We have to make decisions but we can't quite think
No matter what we feel deep inside now
The drunk are getting drunker and we're on the brink
Ain't that a shame

We're only drinking 'cos there's nothing left
And if we didn't we'd be so depressed
The only thing is now we've got bad breath
(spoken: 'But who cares?')
So we'll have another drink, have another drink, have another drink,
have another drink.

(spoken by Gilbert, pretending to be drunk: 'I've only had a mouthful... I love you... Bye'. *he falls over)*

Child *(being brave and approaching the Stranger)* So what is the Plague Mister?

Stranger It's something you don't want to come face to face with on a dark night.

Child You mean it's ugly like Gilbert.

Gilbert *(looks shocked)* I've got good qualities.

Child 'Course you have Gilbert... just remind us of some of them!

Stranger The Plague's caused by the fleas that live on the black rat. It kills the ignorant and the innocent. They say the only thing to do is to run away from it as far as possible.

Catherine *(gasps)* Oh no! I've just remembered, I promised to meet Thomas tonight.

Alice looks at her

Don't worry Alice. I know what I'm doing. I'm going to tell him that I'm staying here. *(she exits)*

Emily *(to the Stranger)* Have you run away then, I mean if the Plague's really that bad in London?

Stranger They dig open pits in London for the bodies... pits the size of your village down there. The streets are narrow and dirty and the rats seek warmth and allow the fleas to feed off them.

Emily How do you know so much?

Stranger *(sharply)* I just do.

Alice So how did the Plague get into our village if the rats are in London?

Stranger *(shrugs)* Packages sent to your village from London, people from the village who visited London and then returned...

Gilbert Or strangers who have visited the village whilst carrying the Plague.

They all look at Gilbert and then at the Stranger. The Stranger leans towards Gilbert who quickly retreats

Emily *(to the Stranger)* <u>You</u> haven't brought it with you have you?

The children back off. The Stranger is definitely not well

Stranger *(struggling)* Look, I don't intend to hurt you, any of you. You've got to believe me. I didn't expect to find anyone out here. I just needed to get away.

Alice Your eyes are dull Mister, are you sure you're alright?

Emily Did something happen in London that forced you to leave?

The Stranger says nothing, Emily looks at him

Emily You've got the Plague haven't you?

Stranger *(remembering)* I lifted water to her lips and I changed the foul bedding in which she lay... *(all the children look at each other)* She said the air smelt sweet yet I smelt nothing.

Alice Who? Who are you talking about? Is this the girl I remind you of? Is that why you keep looking at me?

Stranger I buried her with my own hands. I couldn't even look at her. She was so beautiful and yet I couldn't even bring myself to look at her. *(he pauses)* And they blamed me... in their ignorance her family blamed me for her death. *(he looks at Alice)* And how you remind me of her Alice!

Alice Was she your daughter?

Stranger *(he looks at her)* My wife.

Emily You don't look well anymore Mister. It's your eyes, they don't smile like other people's. Even Jenkins the gravedigger has smiley eyes.

Stranger Don't worry about me little one, I just need to rest.

Alice Look, it's been a long day for all of us. We can't stop you from sleeping on the hill tonight, but you're not to come anywhere near us. I'm sorry, it's what we've been told.

Stranger It's alright... I understand. *(he moves to another area. He doesn't look well)*

As the children settle down to sleep the Stranger stands and walks downstage. Alice watches him. He looks down at the village and then at the children. The Stranger then looks up at the sky

Stranger You took my wife, my family, my friends... my life. You force me to run, you force me to keep looking behind. I know you're out there waiting for your chance to take me. Well that's fine because I've got nothing left. But don't touch these children, do you hear me - don't let them feel the pain I've felt. They don't deserve to die.

Song

'WE'LL KEEP RUNNING'

Him Hold a moment in your hand
And try understand
How I feel, how I feel
I recall the things they said
The lies that filled my head
Look at me, look at me
I can see a rainbow, someone else's rainbow

Turn to look, but she's not there
I've lost all those who care
It's too late, it's too late

Please don't touch, let them live
I've nothing else to give
See these hands, empty hands
I can see a rainbow, someone else's rainbow

And I'll keep running, like somebody scared
Frightened of what I might find
And I'll keep running, afraid of the truth
Running no matter how blind
From what I don't understand... I'll keep running

Alice Just close your eyes and I'll be there, someone to hold you
Would it be wrong to share your life, I know you care
You don't need a rainbow, you don't need a rainbow

Just close your eyes and I'll be there, we all need someone
(Sung against first verse)
Forget the past, the hurt you feel, just stay a while
I can see a rainbow, someone else's rainbow
(Unison)
And we'll keep running, like somebody scared
Frightened of what we might find
And we'll keep running, afraid of the truth
Running, no matter how blind
From what we don't understand... We'll keep running

Alice sings part of the song after hearing what he said. During the song the stranger notices that Emily's blanket has fallen off her. He picks it up and places it back over her as she sleeps. He strokes her head

Scene change to the Sisters of Thyme holding candles. They are in three separate windows in the village

Dill And so they sleep.
Lichen Like graves in a graveyard.
Marjoram A sense of doubt.
Lichen A stranger.
Marjoram Unaware that wherever he goes... another will die.
Dill Seeds are sewn.
Lichen Seeds that grow.
Dill Into trees.
Marjoram That bare fruit.
All Forbidden fruit.
Lichen And we have the cure.
Dill And shall it be shared?
All Daa!!! It shall not!

Marjoram Let them suffer.
Dill You care for them really.
Marjoram They grow on you I suppose.
Lichen Yeah, like warts. *(she smiles nastily)*
Dill Let them choke on their ignorance.
Lichen They only had to ask for our help.
Dill And did they?
All They did not!
Lichen So instead we'll keep the cure for ourselves.
All To die or not to die.
Dill That is the question.
Lichen And if we're not the most attractive women in the village, may we be struck down by lightning.
Marjoram *(unsure)* ...struck down by lightning.
Dill *(worried)* ...struck down by lightning.

They wait for lightning, nothing happens

All Daaa!!!
Lichen Sshh... the Plague moves quickly.
Marjoram There's poison in the air.
Dill Let us drink.
Lichen As people sleep.
Dill As they die.
Marjoram Like a candle burning itself out.
All Let them die. *(they blow the candles out)*

Scene change to Abby standing by the gates looking into the village. She is standing alone

Abby All I want to do is go home. Please understand. I want to see my parents again and hold them. I can't stand it up here anymore. I know that if I enter the village I may die... I know that! So please look after Emily and the others for me.

Song

'LETTING GO'

I've looked out of windows, I've wished on the moon
That someone out there loves me

Life, isn't always as you want it
Dreams, are not often as they seem
But I know inside
There's a feeling, I'm trying to hide

Can anybody help me?
Lost, are the days that I remember
Gone, are the things I should have said
Now you're out of reach
And in the end there's only me
But I won't let it go

> Letting Go
> A boat on the ocean, let it go
> I'll cry and then you'll know how much I miss you
> A feeling you never will know
> You will never know, never know
> When letting go

Why can't I run and be beside you (How I look out at the stars and ask)
What, would you say if I was there (Where are you now?)
For I'm not afraid
I think of you each Summers day
And I can't let it go

> Letting Go
> A boat on the ocean, let it go
> I'll cry and then you'll know how much I miss you
> A feeling you never will know
> You will never know, never know
> When letting go

I tried to say how much I need you, tried to hold you in my heart
Opened up my eyes but you weren't there

(Repeat Chorus "Letting Go, A boat...etc" with added counter melody of 'Ring a Ring a Roses')

Full Company appear during the song including Abby's mother who appears in a separate part of the acting area but when Abby walks through the gates into the village her mother disappears

The company sing the final chorus

A villager steps forward as the others exit

Villager As she stood there waiting for her Mother to run out and hold her, Abby realised she was too late, her Mother had died two days earlier.

Abby starts crying and the Villager holds her in a pool of light that slowly fades. She knows she cannot return to her friends

It is early morning and slowly the sun is rising. Suddenly Gilbert sits up, he was having a nightmare

Roland What... what is it Gilbert?
Gilbert It was just a nightmare about all the animals in the world dying.

The other children have gathered around

Child That's sad...
Roland I got sad when I thought I'd lost my pet sheep, Grape! *(he stands)*
Alice You called a sheep Grape?!
Roland It was when he <u>first</u> died.
Child When he first died?
Roland Yeah!
Child So he's died twice?
Roland No! Three times
Alice And he came back to life each time?!
Roland Yeah, even after we buried it!
Gilbert How did he look each time he came back to life?
Roland Oh he always looked a bit different, but then what do you expect... he <u>had</u> died!
Alice Er Roland? You don't think that perhaps your caring, but totally insane mother simply got you another sheep each time and called it Grape so as you wouldn't be upset?
Roland So poor Grape did actually die then? And the other two Grapes as well? *(he looks upset)*
Gilbert I would say the whole bunch of Grapes died! *(he laughs)*
Roland Oh no!!
Gilbert And each time they died... (he chuckles) ...they gave out a little 'wine'!

They all laugh as Catherine enters back on and one of the children notices that Emily isn't well

Child Alice? I don't think Emily's well, she keeps saying that she's hot and then she says she's cold! I think she's got a fever.
Alice *(realising)* Oh no! Please no! *(she rushes over to Emily)*
Emily It's okay Alice, I don't feel any pain.

The Stranger realises that Emily has the beginnings of the Plague

Stranger Why? Why is it that everywhere I go someone dies. *(he looks up)* Is this the price I'm expected to pay. They're children... they're only children! I'll not hang around to see the consequences - do you hear me. You can't make me suffer again. There is no way I'm gonna take the blame this time. I'm sorry Alice.

Alice You've given her the Plague haven't you... haven't you?

Alice goes to hit him but is held back by the others. The Stranger throws
the silver cross to the floor and exits

Catherine What's happening Alice, why is everything going wrong?
Alice What do you mean?
Catherine He wasn't there. We arranged to meet by the stream and Thomas
didn't turn up. I waited all night Alice. He wouldn't just not turn up. He's
dead isn't he... Thomas is dead!
Alice Oh no, don't say that Catherine.
Catherine But he promised.

A light comes up on Thomas in the village. The children freeze around
Emily during the song. Catherine and Alice sing part of the song

Song

'I'LL BE HERE WAITING FOR YOU'

In my life, I've never seen
One like her who touches me
No one knows how good it's been
Once upon a Summers dream

Is it wrong to love him so
Should I stay or should I go
Deep inside he'll never know
Face the truth and tell him so

Take your time, don't be rushed
Make the choice you have to make
If you feel it's all too much
Close your eyes, try again
And I'll be here waiting for you

Don't throw away what we've been through will you
This is the time when your dreams come true for you
Don't turn your back on the ones you care for
Each day's a new Summer's day

Take your time, don't be rushed
Make the choice you have to make
If you feel it's all too much
Close your eyes, try again
And I'll be here waiting for you

A girl whose face is smiling, a girl whose love I've found
My world is turning around

Don't throw away what we've been through will you *(sung against verse 1)*
This is the time when your dreams come true for you
Don't turn your back on the ones you care for *(sung against verse 2)*
Each day's a new Summers day

Take your time, don't be rushed
Make the choice you have to make
If you feel it's all too much
Close your eyes, try again
And I'll be here waiting for you

Peter enters with Geoffrey. He stands on the stile. As the children are crowding around Emily who is lying in a pool of light

Peter No need to fear... Peter is here! Well, did you miss me?

They just look at him

Well?!

Alice Emily's not well Peter... I think, I think she's got the Plague.

Peter What are you talking about? How can she get the Plague? She hasn't been anywhere!

Gilbert I reckon it was the Stranger.

One of the children sees the cross on the floor and picks it up

Alice No! Don't say that... we don't know that for sure!

Peter What Stranger? *(he looks around)* What are you lot talking about?

Child Alice, it looks like he's taken Abby with him.

Alice No! He wouldn't do that! He would never hurt us, not one purpose. He liked us, I know
he did, I heard him say. He was just lonely and trying to make something of what was left of his life.

Peter Well, who was he then? And where's Abby?

Roland We dunno who he was Peter... he just sort of appeared.

Child Maybe Abby's gone back to the village. She was missing her mum.

Alice Abby wouldn't just leave.

Peter Good job I'm back I reckon.

Roland I didn't see any boils on him Peter.

Gilbert Ah yeah! But he did know a lot about the verkin!

Roland Vermin, Gilbert... it's vermin.

Gilbert Yeah and that!

Peter You only need to take a look at Emily to see what he was... use your eyes. He was the Plague alright.

Emily I'm cold Alice.

Alice *(holding Emily)* You're going to be fine Emily, we are not going to let you die.

Peter *(to Alice)* I hope you realise it's all your fault.

Alice just looks harshly at him

Emily *(struggling)* I'm not scared of dying Alice and please don't blame yourself.

The children freeze as Emily steps from the pool of light as if dead. They continue to look to where she was lying

Song

'GOODBYE CHILDREN'

When day has turned to night, close your eyes
And when things will be alright, find the light
But don't ask me how I feel inside
I won't know what to say

You don't know what you've got, 'til it's gone
And I promised you the world, I was wrong
So don't ask me how I feel inside
I've never felt so cold

So Goodbye Children
Let the dreamers sleep
As still as a boat at sea
So rest now children
Summer days to keep
And sleep for a chance to dream

As the music continues... Emily takes three steps backwards and turns into the darkness. The children then stand, take three steps backwards and turn into the darkness leaving Catherine staring at the pool of light. Sheldon rushes on and falls to his knees. The music stops suddenly

Sheldon *(screaming)* No! No! *(he starts to cry)* It was me wasn't it, I made her die 'cos I done some gravedigging. It's all my fault. *(he looks at the area where Emily had been lying)* I'm sorry.... I'm sorry lady. I liked you I did. You was the only real friend I had.

An unaccompanied voice can be heard singing,
> I've looked out of windows,
> I've wished on the moon,
> That someone out there loves me"

Only Sheldon and Catherine remain on stage. Catherine steps forward with gentle piano music playing a reprise of 'Letting Go' under her final speech

Catherine You just feel an emptiness when someone dies and you think of things you wish you had said. I was dry-eyed at Emily's graveside. I couldn't cry for trembling. Yet in my mind I kept wanting to tell Emily all about it as though I could turn round and see her standing beside me., but she wasn't there.

When the Plague was over and the village pronounced safe, we were told that most of the children on the hill survived with only a few catching the virus after Emily's death. I even saw Thomas again. The saddest news was that Abby had died several days after re-entering the village to see her parents and as for the Stranger no one knows!

It was a time for adventure, a time to build friendships and confront fears. It was a time when the story was told, the last word given.

Catherine turns and exits, leaving Sheldon kneeling alone

Jenkins the gravedigger enters pushing a cart with the three Sisters of Thyme lying in it

Sheldon Hello Mister, where's your shovels?
Jenkins It's all over now boy
Sheldon Where's Nunwin then?
Jenkins Oh! Sad that! He complained of toothache, so I buried him! Got a nice shirt out of it though! *(he opens his jacket to reveal Unwin's shirt with the four pitchfork holes in)*
Sheldon So what have you got in the cart then Mister Jenkins? *(he stands to have a look)*
Jenkins The three Hags who lived in the village.
Sheldon Did the Plague get them as well?
Jenkins No! They was struck by lightning.
Dill *(sighs)* Struck by lightning!
Marjoram *(sighs)* Struck by lightning!
Lichen *(sighs)* Struck by lightning!
Sheldon Oh! *(he goes to exit)*
Jenkins Hang about boy... how do you fancy being my new apprentice?

Sheldon spits on his hand and shakes Jenkins' hand

Get the cart!

Jenkins turns to the audience and winks but then realises that Sheldon is having problems lifting the cart. Jenkins hits him round the head and they both pull the cart off together

The company enter slowly to sing the final chorus number

Song

'IF ONLY FOR THE CHILDREN'

Hear how our hearts are beating
See how we stand tall
We will be brave now
Cry no tears, we'll not fall

From every hope we're given
Fires will keep burning
Days we'll remember
In our hearts, not broken

> And we'll be strong
> And we'll give more
> And we will sing this song forever
> And we will stand (we will be strong)
> Stand side by side (we will be strong)
> And fight once more another day

If only for the children *(counter melody:* We must be strong for the children)
We'll show no fear now
Finding the best way
We will live a new day

From every hope we're given
Fires will keep burning
Days we'll remember
To fight once more another day

Finale/Walkdown

'MEDLEY'

A Ring of Roses

by
Darren Vallier

Superb
'Original Cast Recording'
CD

21 songs from the show

Music arranged by Paul Heard
Produced by Simon Morris
Performed by Starlite Theatre Group
£12

All of Darren Vallier's other published work
including

'When Saturday Comes'
'Two Mini Pantos'
'The Darren Vallier Songbook'
"The Garden Plot and The Ivory Forest'

now available from
Jasper Publishing